MISSISSIPPI DELTA FINGERSTYLE SOLOS
MADE EASY
BY LARRY McCABE

Online Audio   www.melbay.com/99566BCDEB

Audio Contents

1 2 3 4 5 6 7 8 9 0

Table of Contents

Introduction

Many blues scholars think blues fingerpicking originated in the Mississippi Delta, but there were also strong Negro blues traditions in Texas, the Carolinas, and other locations in the Jim Crow South. In fact, there is no way to know precisely where the first fingerstyle blues solo was played, much less who played it. What is important is that, from the time of its inception, blues fingerpicking has endured to become a mainstay on the acoustic music landscape. As we enter the new century, the fingerpicking blues guitar style maintains a healthy following of enthusiastic devotees–pickers and fans–who stubbornly resist the ever-encroaching, powerful electronic entertainment industry that labors daily to eradicate all music associated with tradition, individualism, originality, and feeling.

When I started playing in the 1960s there were very few blues fingerpicking instruction books available (my main "instruction book" was a reel-to-reel tape recorder, slowed down to half-speed). Today, transcriptions are available on almost all the major blues guitarists; still, the beginner is often understandably bewildered by the complex picking patterns and eccentric rhythms played by developed stylists. As a result, the folks at Mel Bay asked me to prepare a collection of easy Mississippi Delta blues fingerpicking solos for you pickers who are just getting started. We have endeavored here to provide arrangements that are easy to understand, technically accessible, and fun to play.

It is our sincere hope that this book will "blow the blues away" from the learning process, and help make the sun shine in your back door someday.

Larry McCabe

Boones Mill, Virginia

How to Use This Book

The Written Music

1. The songs and examples in this book are arranged in the *two-part* guitar notation style. In general, the melody part is written with the stems up, while the bass part is written with the stems down.

    Most of the bass notes are played with the thumb of the picking hand; exceptions are indicated in the music.

2. Each example is also written in tablature for non-readers, and for clarification of fretting positions.

3. Notation symbols are explained on page 30.

4. With the exception of "Salty Dog Blues," which is played in "straight time," all the music in this book should be played using *swing eighths*.

    Please see the explanation on page 31 if you are unfamiliar with the concept of swing eighths.

Technique

1. Suggested fretting-hand fingerings are provided in the notation staff. The recommended fingerings are not absolute, and you can modify a particular fingering if you have a better idea.

    1 = First finger; 2 = Second finger; 3 = Third finger; 4 = Fourth finger

2. Fingerpickers often *mute* the bass to create a percussive accompaniment sound. To mute the bass, cover the low E, A and D strings with the side of the picking hand near the bridge.

3. Performance notes and helpful chord and fingering diagrams accompany each song.

The Companion CD

1. A long "A" tuning beep is provided on track 1 of the companion CD.

2. The CD, recorded in stereo, is mixed as follows:
    The drums are on the <u>left</u> channel.
    The **guitar** is on the <u>right</u> channel.

3. Although fingerpicking blues is usually played without drums, you will find that the inclusion of drums on the CD will help you with the timing of the music. If you wish, you may remove either the guitar or the drums by turning down the appropriate speaker.

4. Each song is recorded twice–the first time at slow speed, then at medium speed.

Procedure

Be sure to study the <u>Guide to Symbols</u> on pages 30.

The first two solos, "Mudslide Blues" and "Canepole Catfish," are the easiest songs in the book. Learn these first, then work through the rest of the material in any order. If you encounter an example that is too difficult, try a different song, then return to the more challenging piece later.

"Mudslide Blues"

"Mudslide Blues" is a great first solo…it's almost all open strings!

- This song is a *twelve-bar blues*. Twelve-bar blues is the most popular blues form, with the majority of all blues songs being twelve bars in length.

- The bass line (stems down) is in the *alternating bass* style. Most alternating bass parts consist of a note on each beat. This simplified arrangement contains a bass note every other beat. This will help you learn the technique of alternating bass in an easy manner.

- In fingerpicking, it is not always necessary to hold down "complete" chord forms, even if the chord symbols appear in the music. "Mudslide Blues" uses only the chord "fragments" shown in the above diagrams. This makes things easy on the fretting hand.

- This song is based on simple picking patterns; there is no distinct melody here. Pick the treble (stems up) notes with either your index or middle finger.

The Chord Diagrams

- X means "do not play this string." No fingers are required on these strings.

- 0 means "play this string open."

- Fretting fingers are numbered as follows:
    - 1 = first finger (index finger)
    - 2 = second finger (middle finger)
    - 3 = third finger (ring finger)
    - 4 = fourth finger (pinky)

- We do not strum these chords. Instead, we pick out the bass and treble parts, as shown in the music/tab on the next page.

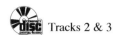

Mudslide Blues

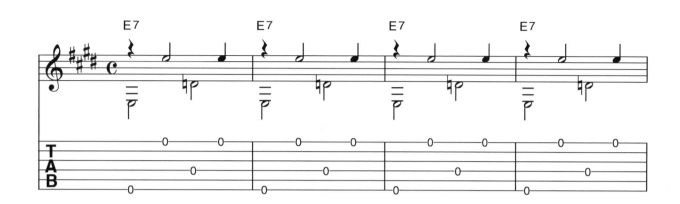

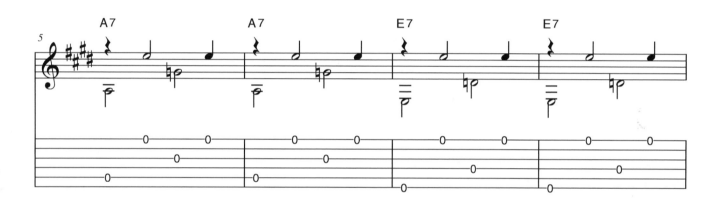

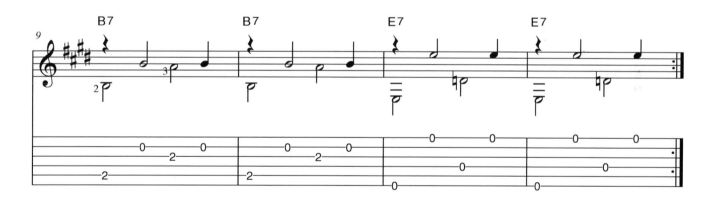

"Canepole Catfish"

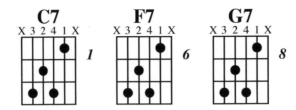

"Canepole Catfish" uses the same picking pattern in each measure, but the chord fingering (or shape) is played at different frets throughout the tune.

• Play the alternating bass line (stem down) with the thumb.

• The m-i-m picking pattern (see measure one) is used for the high part (stems up) throughout the tune.

Chord Shapes

The C7 chord shape is used for all three chords in "Canepole Catfish." Fret each chord according to the fingerings shown above the chord grids. Start with C7:

   • The first finger (index) frets the second string
   • The fourth finger (little) frets the third string
   • The second finger (middle) frets the fourth string
   • The third finger (ring) frets the fifth string

Reminder: The "x" (above strings one and six) means "do not play this string." No fingers are required on these strings. Play only strings 2, 3, 4, and 5.

The number to the right side of each grid shows the lowest fret in each chord. Play C7 at frets 1-3; F7 is played at frets 6-8; and G7 is played at frets 8-10.

• A chord with no open strings is called a *closed chord*. Closed chords are moveable shapes that can be played on any root tone. For example, if you play the above chord shape at frets 3-5 you will have a D7 chord (D7 is a whole step, or two frets, above C7). **Another example:** An E7 chord could be played by forming this chord shape at frets 5-7.

Canepole Catfish

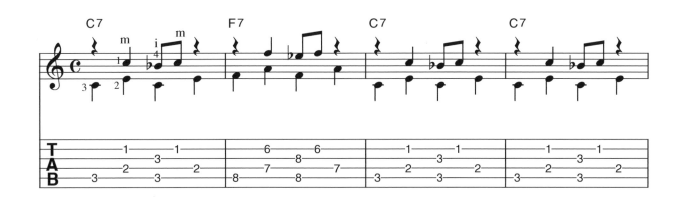

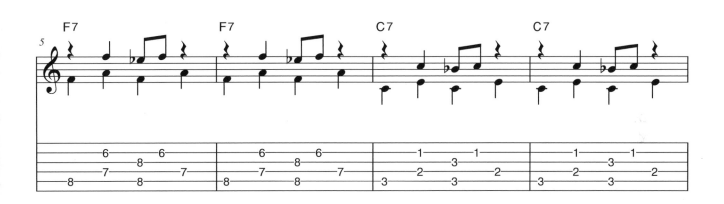

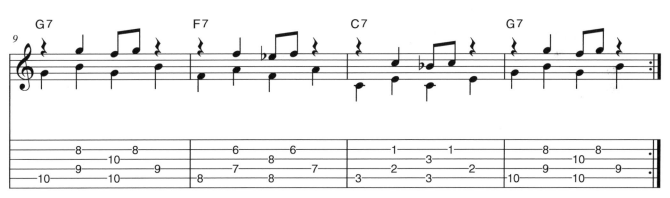

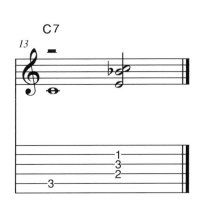

7

"Zuba"

"Zuba," like "Canepole Catfish," uses the same picking pattern in every measure. In this song, however, open-string chords are used.

- "Zuba" uses the basic D7 and A7 chords. The basic G7 chord is slightly modified for this arrangement.

- The following open strings, though shown on the chord grids, are not actually played in this song:

    - The open fifth string of D7
    - The open third string of G7
    - The open third string of A7

However, it is easier to leave these strings open than to try to mute them.

- Mute the fifth string of G7 by slightly leaning the ring finger in the direction of this string, so that the flesh of the finger lightly touches the string. This is a standard muting technique for this chord.

- The bass notes (stems down) are played with the thumb as follows:

    - The bass for D7 is strings 4 / 3
    - The bass for G7 is strings 6 / 4
    - The bass for A7 is strings 5 / 4

- It is often a good idea to first practice the bass (low) part in isolation, before attempting the treble (high) part. This usually makes it easier to learn the bass and treble parts simultaneously.

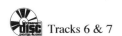
Zuba

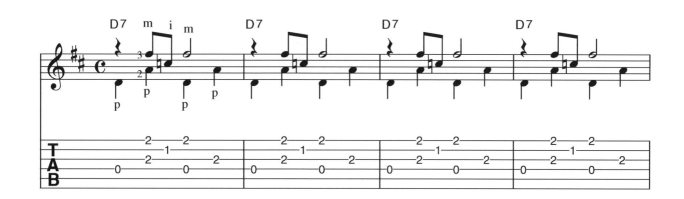

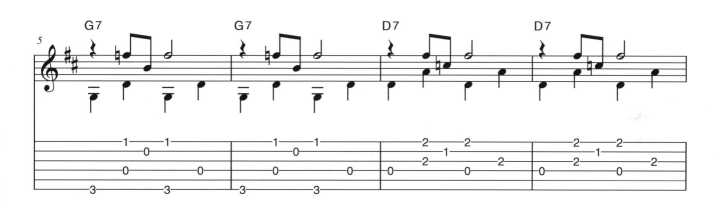

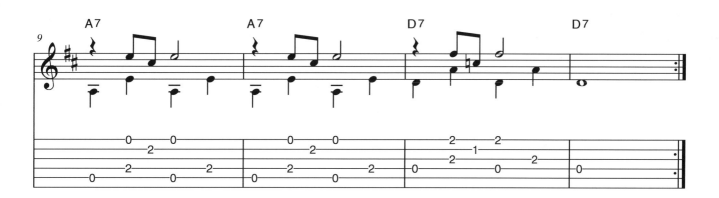

"Backwater Blues"

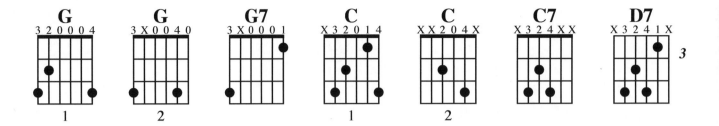

The vocal-like melody of "Backwater Blues" requires the fretting hand to "slip around" many of the chord forms. If you are accustomed to playing mostly strummed rhythm guitar, your concept of chords will be expanded quite a bit while you learn to fingerpick. In fingerpicking, the fretting hand is often "on the move," and not "glued down" to the chord of the moment.

- No picking-hand fingerings are suggested for this song. Drawing on your current fingerpicking experience, work out the picking according to what feels right to you. **Tip:** Traditional players often use the index finger for most of the treble notes, with the middle finger used to help with runs of successive eighth notes.

- The following performance notes will help prepare your fretting hand for our arrangement. Measure numbers do not include the pickup measure; measure 1 means the first full measure.

G Chord

- Measure 1: The first beat is played with form 1, minus the middle finger. The third beat is played with form 2, minus the middle finger.

- Measures 3-4, 7-8, 11-12: Keep the third finger "planted" on the sixth string while playing the bass line in these measures.

G7 Chord

- Measures 1 and 5: A little piece of the G7 chord is used on the second beat of each of these measures. There is no need to hold down any notes in the chord that are not played.

C7 Chord

- Measures 2 and 6: Lift the fourth finger after playing the first beat in each of these measures.

- Measure 10: Lift the little finger after playing the melody note on the third beat.

C Chord

- Measure 5: Use strings five and one from form 1 on the first beat; form 2 is used on the second beat. The technical name for form 2 is "C add 9."

D7 Chord

- Measure 9: Play the D7 chord as shown in the grid above.

Backwater Blues

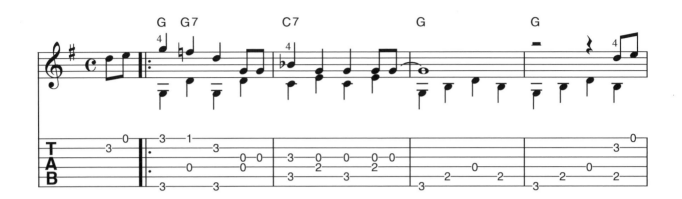

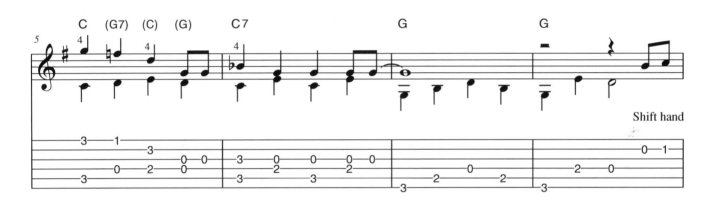

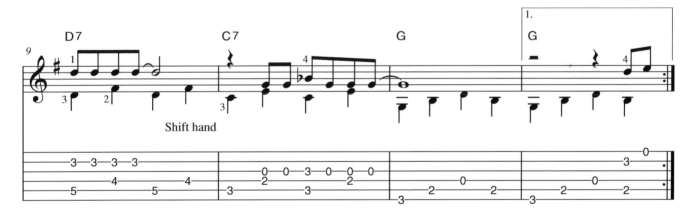

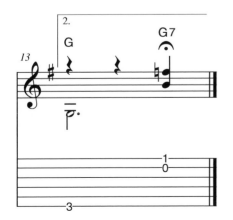

"Red Pineapple Blues"

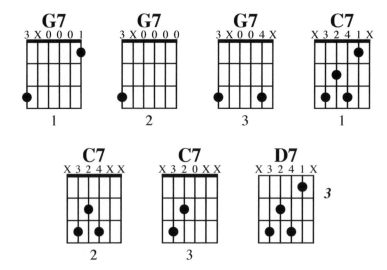

"Red Pineapple Blues" contains a fair amount of *syncopation* in the form of melody notes being played on offbeats. Nonetheless, the song should be fairly easy to play if you study the music carefully before attempting to play the whole song.

A good way to get started would be to go over the following notes on the chord positions:

G7 Chord in Measures 1 and 2

1. Begin with form **1**.

2. *Pull* ("snap") the index finger away from the first string to play form **2**.

3. Add the little finger (4) to the second string to play form **3**.

G7 Chord in Measures 3 and 7

Follow instructions for measures 1 and 2 (above), then…

4. Remove the little finger from the second string to play form **2** again.

C7 Chord in Measures 5 and 6

1. Begin with form **1,** playing the bass line plus the treble note on the second string.

2. Pluck the third fret of the third string (see form **2**). It's o.k. to leave your first finger on the second string (see form **1**) while doing this if you wish.

3. Remove your little finger from the third fret to play the open third string. Again, you can leave the first finger down on the second string if you wish.

D7 Chord in Measures 9 and 12

The D7 chord form shown above is used in measures 9 and 12. There is no motion in the fretting hand while this chord is played.

After playing D7 in measure 9, *shift* down two frets to play the C7 chord.

Red Pineapple Blues

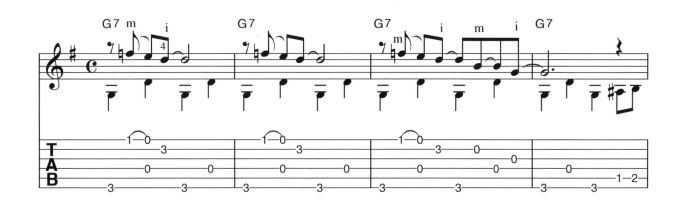

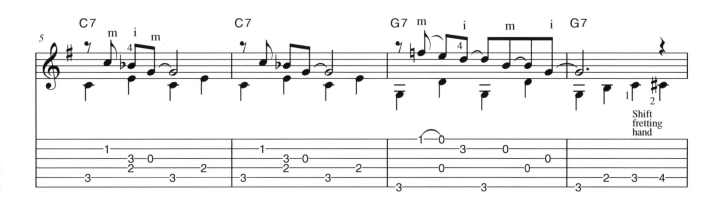

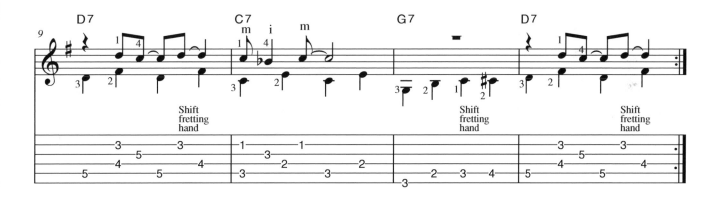

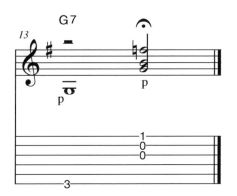

"Mississippi Moan"

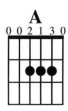

"Mississippi Moan" is based on typical blues melody lines heard in many songs.

• <u>Practice the melody line separately before adding the bass.</u> Listen closely to the CD, humming with the melody, to make sure your concept of the melody is accurate. Make up words for the melody if this will help you memorize the melody.

A Chord

• The only chord form that is held down in this song is the A chord (see above).

• Measure 1: Add the little finger to the second string, third fret, on the "2 and" beat. Remove the little finger on the third beat.

D7 Chord

• Measures 2, 5, and 6: The descending melody notes E-D-C-A do not require a "fixed" hand position.

• The bass for D7 is very simple, requiring only an alternation of the fifth and fourth strings, respectively.

E7 Chord

• Measures 9 and 10: The fretting hand is kept "free" (no fixed chord forms) for both E7 measures. The bass is a simple monotone bass on the sixth string.

• Measure 10: Slide the ring finger to the fifth fret of the first string on the first beat. Shift the fretting hand back to the basic position after playing the open first string melody note.

Mississippi Moan

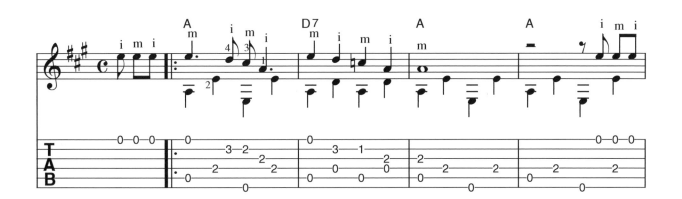

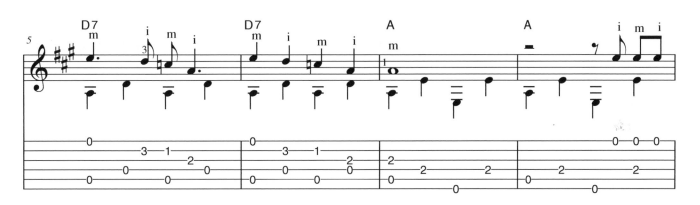

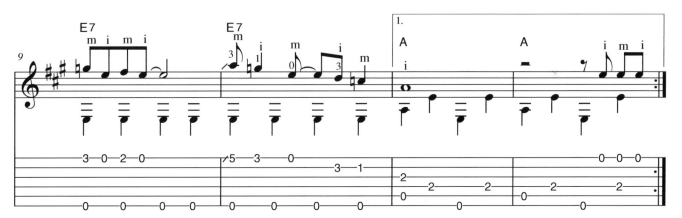

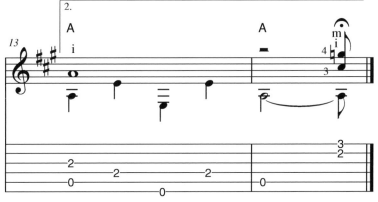

"Bullfrogs for Breakfast"

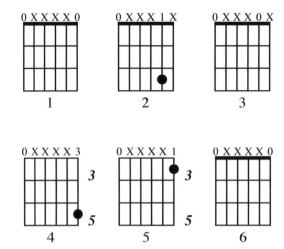

"Bullfrogs for Breakfast" is an *eight-bar blues*. "Key to the Highway," "Stagger Lee," and "Trouble in Mind," all blues standards, are also in the eight-bar form. "Bullfrogs for Breakfast" is a *monochord* (one chord) song, using only the E7 chord.

• Although the harmony is E7 throughout, we never actually hold down an E7 chord in this arrangement. You might say we're working around E7.

• Measures 1-5 are played in the *third position*. Have your first finger on or near the third fret of the second string (see form 2, above) when you start the song.

• The chord forms above (#1-6) show the playing positions for the first five measures:

     • Measure 1: Play form 1, then form 2, then form 3 (see the music/tab, next page).
     • Measure 2 Is the same as measure 1.
     • Measure 3: All six forms are used in this measure, in numerical order (1-6). Play a *pull-off* to get from form 4 to form 5.
     • Measure 4 is bass only, but leave the fretting hand in third position.
     • Measure 5 is the same as measure 1 and 2.

• Shift the fretting hand to basic position in measure 7. Fret the third fret of the second string with the ring finger.

• If necessary, isolate and practice separately the pull-offs in measures 3 and 7.

Bullfrogs for Breakfast

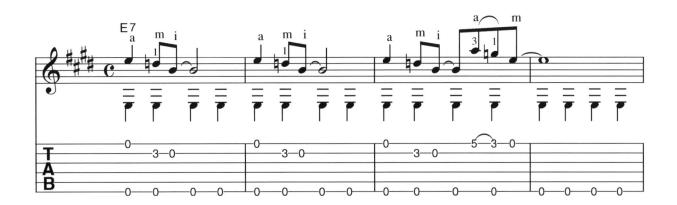

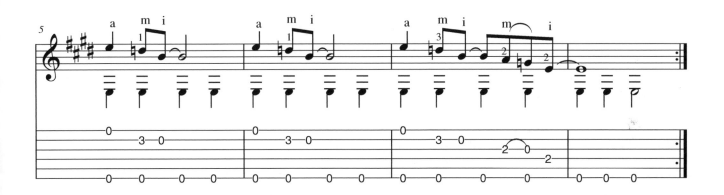

17

"Salty Dog Blues"

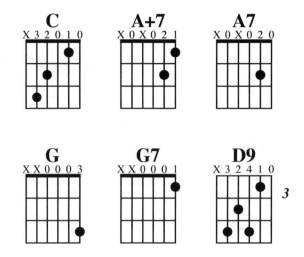

Let me be your Salty Dog,
Or I won't be your man at all;
Honey, let me be your Salty Dog.

"Salty Dog Blues" is a "hokum" blues–lively, and usually accompanied by wry, humorous lyrics. The great Memphis jug bands of the Depression era played many hokum songs. In fact, most every well-known blues musician plays at least one song in this style; Robert Johnson's contribution was called "They're Red Hot."

•   There is quite a bit of syncopation in this song, in the form of upbeat melody notes. However, the simple picking patterns will feel quite natural once you have practiced them diligently.

A+7 Chord (A "augmented" seventh)

•   Measure 2: Start the measure with this chord, then lift the first finger from the first string on the "2 and" beat to produce the A chord.

D9 Chord

•   Measures 3 and 4: Hold this form down and play the picking pattern as shown in the notation. Shift smoothly down to G after playing D9.

G7 Chord

•   Measure 6: There is some left-hand movement "around the chord" here. Lift the first finger so that the melody note on the first beat is played on the open first string, then hammer from the open string to the first fret.

Add the little finger to the third fret, second string on the "3 and" beat.

Be sure to see the bass variation, written below the music on the following page, for measures 5-6.

Salty Dog Blues

Traditional "Hokum" Blues

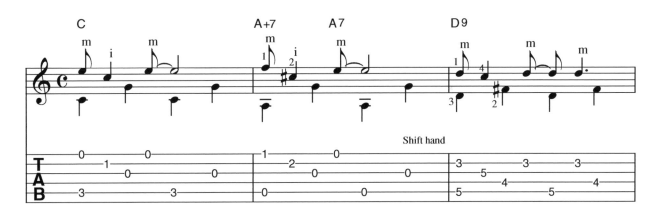

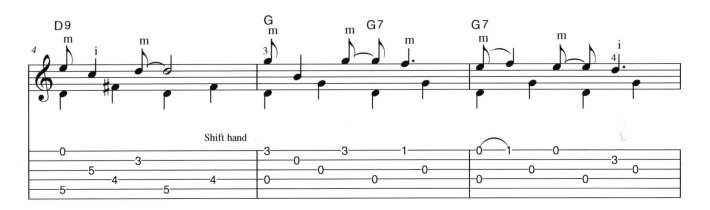

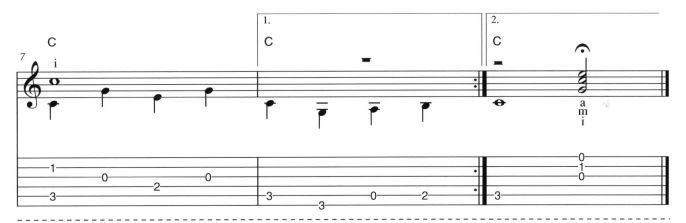

Variation: the following bass line
may be used in measures 5-6. If you
use this bass line, fret the notes on
the third fret with the pinky.

"Saint James Infirmary"

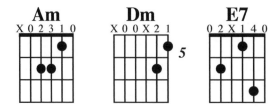

"Saint James Infirmary," also known as "Gambler's Blues," is a *minor-key* blues in the eight-bar form. The following arrangement, played in A minor, uses the three main chords in the key: Am, Dm, and E7.

Although there is nothing real tricky here, the following notes will help you get your fretting hand ready to play the solo. References to measure numbers refer to full measures; the pickup measure (the incomplete measure at the beginning) is cited as such.

Am Chord

• Pickup measure: Hold down the Am chord <u>before</u> you play the pickup notes.

Dm Chord

• Measure 3: Shift the fretting hand from the Am chord to the fifth position to play the Dm chord. This is a "fingerpicking" Dm chord–a "partial chord," if you will–and you need only play the strings shown on the above grid. Be sure not to play the open third string, or the chord will <u>really</u> sound out of tune.

E7 Chord

All the measures that use this chord require only a partial fingering of the form shown above.

• Measure 1: It is not necessary to hold down the third string for E7 in this measure.

• Measure 4: No need to fret any notes here, except the notes in the bass fill-in.

• Measure 5: Same as measure 1–no need to fret the first fret on the third string.

• Measures 7 and 9: No need to use the little finger on the second string.

Picking-Hand Tips

• The picking-hand thumb can play all the bass notes (stems down). **Variation:** Beginning on the second beat of the fourth full measure, play the bass notes in that measure "claw-style": p-i-p-i-p-i.

• Many blues players would use only the index and middle fingers to pick the melody notes. Remember, the picking-hand fingerings shown in the notation are only suggestions.

Saint James Infirmary

Traditional Blues Song

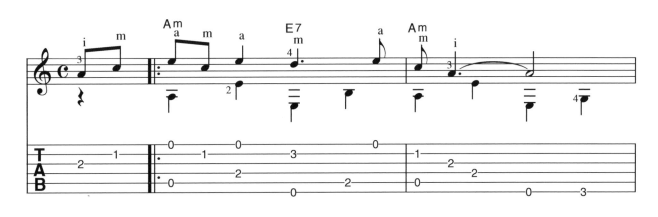

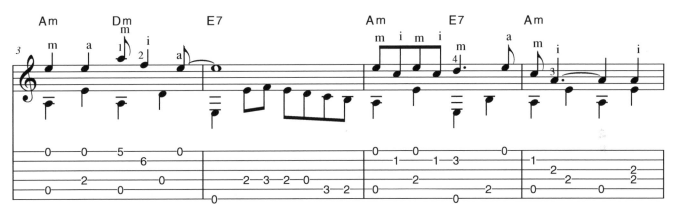

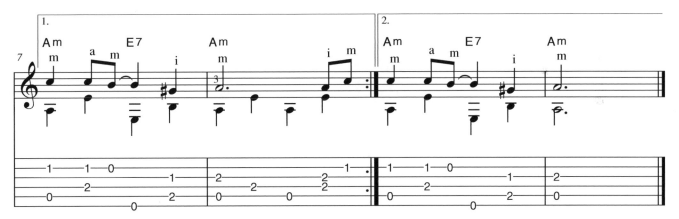

One-Chord Blues Styles in E

A number of Mississippi-style blues use only one chord throughout the song. These one-chord blues songs are often played in either E or E minor, keys which can produce a rather "dark" and ominous sound. The harmony (chord) in the examples below is written as E7, but it actually wavers somewhere between E7 and Em.

Shakedown in Natchez

Tracks 20 & 21

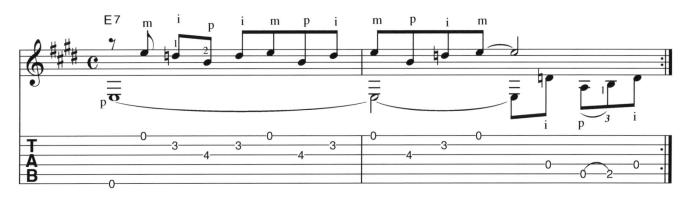

1. The picking-hand pattern is shown as most traditional blues fingerpickers would play it. You can also play a-m-i (ring-middle-index) for the "reverse roll" pattern on strings 1-2-3.

2. *Hammer* from the open A string to the B note on the last beat of the second measure. Review the Symbols Guide if you are not familiar with this technique.

Howlin' in the Canebrake

Tracks 22 & 23

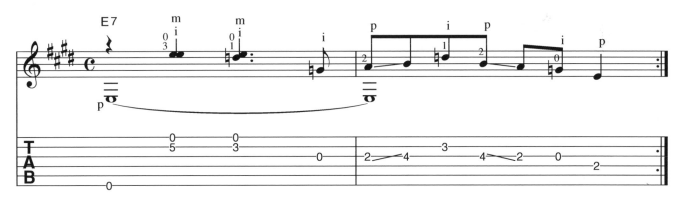

1. The *double-stops* (two strings played at the same time) on beats 2 and 3 of measure one are *pinched* with the middle and index fingers.

2. The remaining melody notes (stems up) are played "claw style" with the index finger and thumb of the picking hand.

3. The diagonal line indicates a *slide*. Be sure to review the Symbols Guide (page 30) if you are unfamiliar with this technique.

"Careless Love"

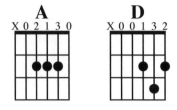

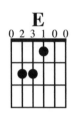

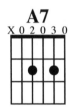 

"Careless Love" has been a favorite of jazz and blues musicians for generations. It is also well-known among folk and bluegrass pickers. W.C. Handy, the "Father of the Blues," called his adaptation of the song "Loveless Love."

- Fingerings for the picking hand are given in the "modern" style. Many blues fingerpickers would pick all the melody notes with only the index finger. Others would use a combination of the middle and index fingers.

- Notice the little "fill-in" licks in measures 8 and 16. Though simple, the fill-ins help to avoid the monotony of playing only the alternating bass for an extended period.

- The A13 chord (above) is played at the end of the song.

Please note the following modifications for the A and D chords:

A Chord

- Measures 5 and 9, fourth beat: Add the little finger on the third fret of the second string. This finger can be removed on the next beat.

- Measure 6, third beat: Add the little finger on the second fret of the first string. Remove the finger on the next beat.

D Chord

- Measure 12, fourth beat: Remove the third finger from the second string, and play the string open.

Careless Love

Traditional Country Blues

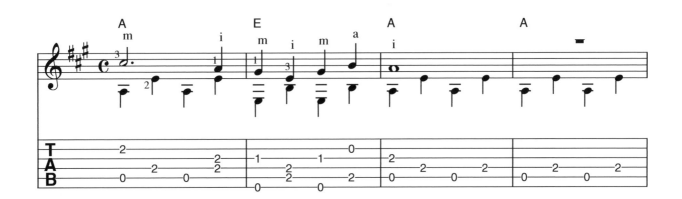

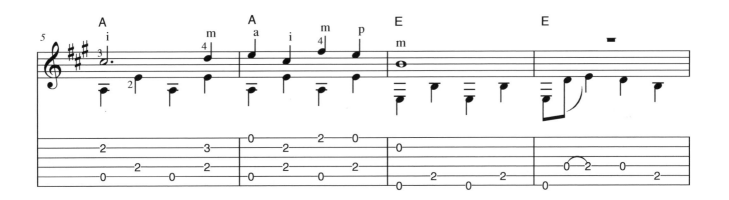

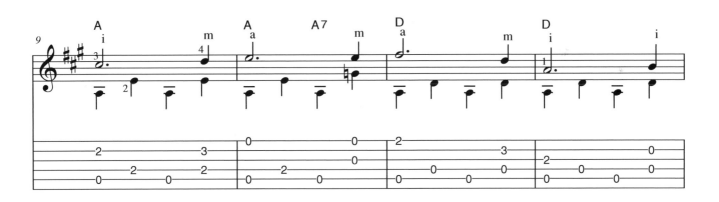

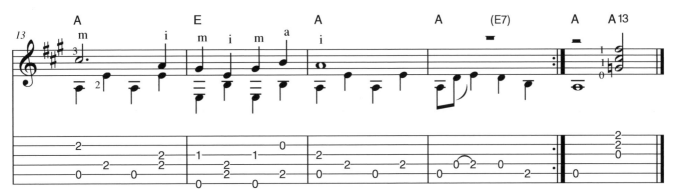

"Midnight Special"

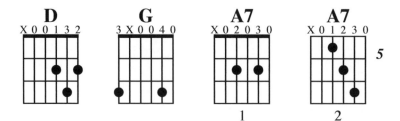

"Midnight Special" has been played and recorded by countless folk, rock, country and blues groups–and even orchestras and gospel quartets. Recorded by Leadbelly, Johnny Rivers, Creedence Clearwater Revival and many others, "Midnight Special" is a great song that is enthusiastically received wherever it is performed.

- To fully understand the music, learn to study the arranging *concepts*. Try to figure out how certain licks can be played in different places, for example. Learn how the chords are built, and be able to name the notes in each chord. A good theory teacher can help you with these fundamentals. Eventually, you will want to apply your knowledge to songs of your own choice.

  By "arranging concepts," we mean things like alternating-bass patterns, chord positions, the use of slurs (hammers, pull-offs, slides, etc.), the phrasing of the melody, the melody and fill-in licks, and so on–in short, just about anything having to do with the creation of the music.

- Don't rush the hammer-ons (pickup measure; measure 8; measure 9). Relax and play in a confident, smooth manner.

- The following comments on the chords will help prepare your fretting hand for our arrangement. Measure numbers do not include the pickup measure; measure 1 means the first <u>full</u> measure.

D Chord

- Measure 4, third beat: Lift the ring finger from the second string so that the open string can be sounded.

- Measure 8: The middle finger must be lifted from the first string on the "2 and" beat, then replaced by hammering from the open string on the third beat.

G Chord

- Measure 1: Lift the little finger from the second string on the "2 and" beat. Replace the finger on the "two and" beat of the following measure.

  G6 is the technical name for a G chord with an open first string.

A7 Chord

- Measure 6: Shift from A7, form 1, to A7, form 2 (see above). Form 2 is technically known as A13, but the notation for thirteenth chords is often simplified in the written music.

Midnight Special

27

Introductions & Turnarounds

The term *turnaround* refers to a chord progression, or chord movement, in the last two bars of a section of music. Not all songs contain turnarounds; "Mudslide Blues," for example (page 5), has only one chord in its last two bars (measures 11-12). We could say that "Canepole Catfish" (page 7) contains a turnaround, since two chords are used in measures 11-12. The turnarounds shown below contain several chords and are closer to what a professional blues guitarist would play.

In blues songs, a turnaround (if used) is played in the following measures:

- Measures 11-12 of a twelve-bar blues.
- Measures 7-8 of an eight-bar blues.
- Measures 15-16 of a sixteen-bar blues.

The following turnaround progressions and licks can be applied to many blues fingerpicking songs, in the measures indicated above. These turnarounds can also be used as two-bar blues *introductions* at the beginning of songs.

Key of G  Track 28

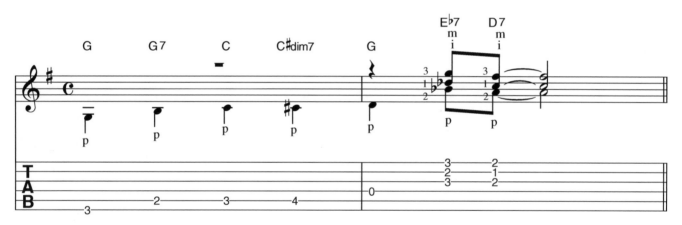

Key of A Track 29

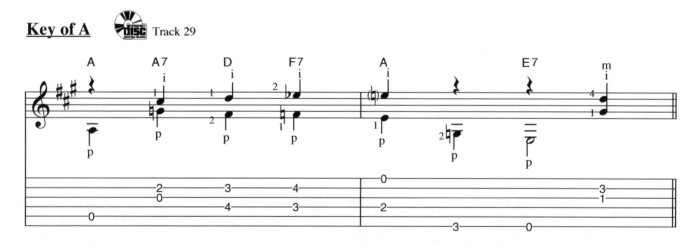

Tip: Enhance your versatility and understanding by learning several fingerings for each chord symbol shown in these turnarounds. You can learn many forms for each chord in Mel Bay's *Deluxe Encyclopedia of Guitar Chords* (93283).

Key of E 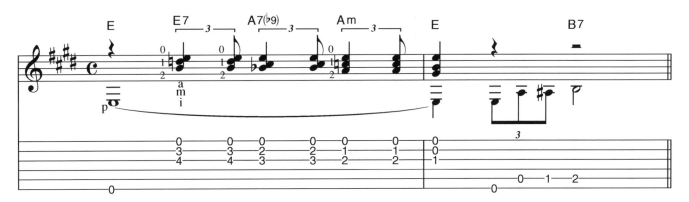 Track 30

Key of C 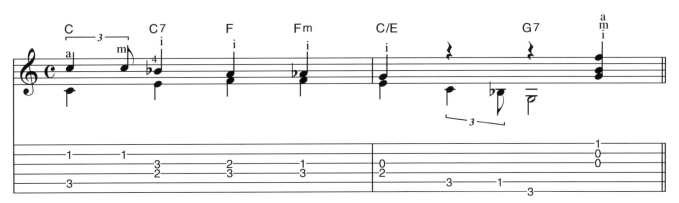 Track 31

Key of D 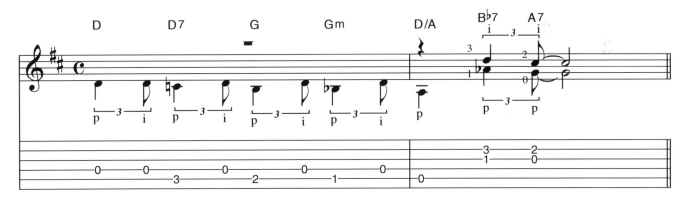 Track 32

For more blues turnaround licks and chord progressions, see the following Mel Bay book/CD sets by Larry McCabe:

- *101 Essential Blues Progressions* (98339BCD).
- *101 Mississippi Delta Blues Fingerpicking Licks* (96241BCD).

Guide to Symbols

Fretting-hand Fingering

1 = First finger (index)
2 = Second finger (middle)
3 = Third finger (ring)
4 = Fourth finger (pinky)
Th = Thumb

Picking-hand Fingering

p = Thumb (pulgar)
i = Index finger (indice)
m = Middle (medio)
a = Ring (anular)

Slurs

Each of the following techniques represents a certain type of slur. A slur causes two (or more) notes to sound with only one "attack." The following slurs (hammers, pulls and slides) are used in this book.

Hammer (or Hammer-on)

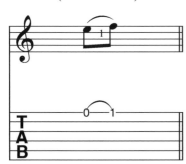

1. Play the open E note with the middle finger of the picking hand.

2. *Hammer* (slam) down the first finger (fretting hand) to sound the F note.

Pull (or Pull-off)

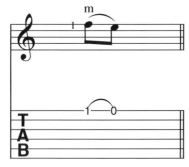

1. Place the first finger of the fretting hand on the F note.

2. Pick the F note with the middle finger of the picking hand.

3. *Pull* the index finger away from the F to sound open E.

   Do not merely lift the finger in a passive manner; instead, pull the finger away from the string with a "snappy" sideways motion.

Slide

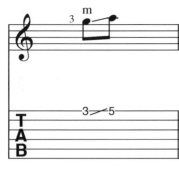

1. Place the third finger of the fretting hand on the G note.

2. Pick the G note with the middle finger of the picking hand.

3. Slide (glide without lifting) the ring finger up the fingerboard to sound the A note.

Tip: Slurs can be combined. For example, it would be possible to strike an open string ("Attack"), hammer to the second fret, then pull-off back to the open string. **Result:** one attack produces three notes.

Swing Eighths

For ease of reading, all of the eighth notes in this book are written in "straight" (or even) time. However, each pair of eighth notes actually sounds like the first and third notes of an eighth-note triplet.* This *swing eighths* effect is a hallmark of blues and jazz rhythms.

The comments that follow will help you understand the timing of swing eighth notes. In addition, listen closely to the companion CD to fully grasp the concept of this rhythm.

Example 1 is written in straight time; however, it sounds like Ex. 2 when interpreted with swing eighths.

When we play Ex. 3 with swing eighths it will sound like Ex. 4.

Tip: Swing eighths may also be called "jazz eighths," lazy eighths," or "shuffle eighths."

****Exception:** "Salty Dog" (page 29) is played in straight time.

Additional Mel Bay Titles by Larry McCabe

- 101 Amazing Jazz Bass Patterns (97336BCD)

- 101 Bad-to-the-Bone Blues Guitar Rhythm Patterns (97760BCD)

- 101 Blues Bass Patterns for Bass Guitar (95330BCD)

- 101 Essential Blues Progressions (98339BCD)

- 101 Essential Country Chord Progressions (99043BCD)

- 101 Essential Rock 'n' Roll Chord Progressions (99182BCD)

- 101 Kickin' Country Rhythm Guitar Runs (98131BCD)

- 101 Red-Hot Jazz-Blues Guitar Licks and Solos (98338BCD)

- 101 Red-Hot Bluegrass Guitar Licks and Solos (99445BCD)

- 101 Red-Hot Bluegrass Mandolin Licks and Solos (99446BCD)

- 101 Red-Hot Swing Guitar Licks (electronic download) (97335D)

- 101 Three-Chord Songs for Guitar, Banjo, and Uke (99476)

- Famous Blues Bass Lines Qwikguide® (98429BCD)

- Famous Guitar Lines Qwikguide® (21142BCD)

- Music Theory 101 (99393)

- You Can Teach Yourself® Song Writing (94823BCD)

Become a **fingerpicking superstar** with this additional Mel Bay title by Larry McCabe:

- **101 Mississippi Delta Blues Fingerpicking Licks** (book/CD set—96241BCD). Without a doubt, the world's finest collection of authentic-sounding blues fingerpicking licks. 4-bar licks, 8-bar licks, turnarounds, and lots of helpful tips. All 101 licks are played at a moderate speed on the companion CD.

Most titles are available as book/CD sets; all guitar and bass books contain both notation and tablature.

Made in the USA
Middletown, DE
17 May 2022

65894596R00020